DWAYNE

JOHNSON

D1527842

Abraham H Garcia

CONTENTS

INTRODUCTION

Dwayne 'The Rock' Johnson, a former professional wrestler, the world's most bankable movie star, and a massively successful entrepreneur, demonstrates that dreams can come true.

However, the path to his triumph was a never-ending uphill battle. The Rock is a man who has been pushed by adversity since he was a child. Dwayne Johnson was evicted from his home at the age of 14, arrested many times by the age of 16, yet he refused to give up.

In a genuine stroke of serendipity, he began playing football by chance in high school, and he discovered his life's love. However, some things in life are simply not meant to be, and at the age of 23, Dwayne Johnson was broke and had to return home to his parents.

His aspirations had been destroyed, but his will was stronger than ever. He was on a new route in life after a few months of soul searching.

Dwayne began his career in professional wrestling as a third-generation superstar, following in the footsteps of his grandfather and father. Despite his hard work and dedication to the industry, the audience rejected him.

Going back to the drawing board and doing some soul searching, The Rock reinvented himself and quickly became one of the biggest performers in professional wrestling history. He won several championships, headlined the most prestigious wrestling events, and had legendary matches. In other words, he had everything.

His heart, however, was aching for a fresh challenge.

The Rock was at the pinnacle of his fame when he embarked on a new journey. He desired to dominate the film industry, becoming a household name and the largest box-office star in Hollywood.

He quickly discovered that Hollywood has an entirely other set of regulations. Because he was the most successful wrestler in his previous life, he had to start from scratch in the brutal world of Hollywood. Whatever you were, you were nothing more than a cog in a well-oiled machine in Hollywood.

It took him a while since he was trying to fit into the mould that Hollywood expected of him. However, Dwayne 'The Rock' Johnson did something no other actor has done before. He became the hottest guy in Hollywood by relying on his personal connection with his followers as well as his wrestling audience.

More than that, The Rock transitioned from an actor to a businessman. He did it with grace, generosity, and his signature bright smile.

We will delve deeper into his ups and downs as we analyse his great achievements in this book.

CHAPTER 1

DWAYNE JOHNSON ORIGIN STORY

Dwayne "The Rock" Johnson's story is one of determination, grit, and good old-fashioned hard work. Rocky Johnson, his father, was a professional wrestler, and the family moved from state to state as Rocky took up bouts wherever he could find work.

The family of three was migrating from state to state, and in fact, they moved quite a bit during Dwayne's formative years. Dwayne had lived in 38 of the 50 states by the time he was a teenager. His father was a hardworking, disciplined professional, and he made certain that his son followed in his footsteps, no matter what he chose to do when he grew up.

Rocky was a traditionalist who taught Dwayne that respect is earned and that he must earn it every day.

Rocky got up between 5:30 and 6:00 a.m. every day, and he would wake up his 5-year-old kid to keep him company in the gym.

Dwayne followed his father to the gym on a daily basis, and by the age of 13, he was lifting weights. Surrounded by huge men at such an early age, the Rock learned the importance of hard work and discipline, which are the exact components required to grow massive and powerful bodies. Being huge and muscular was, in fact, a requirement and part of a wrestler's job description.

Dwayne had previously tried baseball, soccer, martial arts, and gymnastics by the age of eight. What he actually desired was to lift weights. He had to wait a few years before his request was granted.

Dwayne was 13 years old when his father took him to his first workout. The iron's love affair was born. He still goes to the gym every morning at 4:00 a.m., an hour after waking up. However, before we get to the present, we must first handle Dwayne's troubled adolescence.

Rocky Johnson was absent for the most of Dwayne's formative and adolescent years due to the unusual nature of his employment. It was incredibly difficult to be a professional wrestler in the 1970s and 1980s. Wrestlers had to hustle to make ends meet because their jobs were not guaranteed. A pro wrestler is typically on the road for roughly 300 days each year, away from their family as they travel around the country.

Dwayne was lost in life without his father. The family was in financial difficulty since they were living paycheck to paycheck.

The Johnsons were residing in Hawaii in 1986. Dwayne was 14 at the time, and as he and his mother were walking to their home one day, they discovered an eviction notice and a lock on the door. The family became homeless overnight and had to return to the United States.

Dwayne made the decision right then and there that he never wants to be in a powerless situation again. He decided to become someone because he thought the best way to do it was to grow a gigantic body. He desired to place himself in a position where he could influence the course of his life. Dwayne was permanently scarred by seeing the eviction notice and the lock on the door.

Furthermore, he entered the world with a chip on his shoulder from that point forward.

Dwayne had already fallen in love with weightlifting, but from that day on, he became even more dedicated to his daily routine.

Dwayne was arrested for check fraud when he was 15 years old. He had already been arrested for stealing and many fights. When his parents were summoned to the station to pick up their kid, Dwayne recognized that, despite the family's tough circumstances, he was the source of the most stress in their lives.

Despite his decision to change his ways, the young Dwayne's path was not simple.

Dwayne enrolled in Freedom High School in Bethlehem, Pennsylvania, about a year later. A few weeks later, Dwayne's life was drastically altered by an event with a professor.

Dwayne needed to use the restroom one afternoon. Instead of going to the boy's bathroom, he went to the teacher's lounge. A teacher confronted him and ordered him to leave just as he was about to leave.

Dwayne, who was already 6'4 and 220 pounds, refused to leave and instead intimidated the teacher. He couldn't sleep that night, he admitted, since he felt he had done something wrong.

The next day, Dwayne apologised to the teacher for his actions. As he offered his hand to the teacher, it was clear that the young Dwayne genuinely regretted his actions.

The teacher, who turned out to be the high school football coach, saw past the enormous but bewildered kid's rough and tough exterior. Jody Swick, a high school football coach, saw Dwayne's soul, saw his ability, and decided to give him another shot.

He requested that Dwayne play football for him.

Dwayne agreed, unaware that his life was about to change for the better. Dwayne and Jody built a relationship and a special bond over time. Dwayne Johnson still considers Jody Swick to be a father figure and mentor who altered his life. Dwayne transformed himself from an aimless punk child to a devoted professional who found his way in football.

Dwayne's outlook on life and his future shifted as his grades improved and he began to consider his future and objectives. Dwayne's intensity, devotion, and hard work paid off as he began to be recruited by institutions from all across the country.

Dwayne Johnson chose to accept the University of Miami scholarship. In his first year, he led the Miami Hurricanes to the national football championship. Dwayne's future seemed bright as his goals of becoming a pro and playing in the NFL seemed more real than ever.

As fate would have it, his dreams were never realised.

Dwayne suffered a string of ailments after winning the college title. He endured five knee surgeries in a few years, as well as crippling back damage and reconstructive shoulder surgery.

On top of that, Dwayne had the misfortune of facing direct competition for the starting spot in the form of Warren Sapp, a future NFL Hall of Famer and one of the game's finest defensive players.

Dwayne Johnson entered the NFL draft in 1995, but none of the teams elected to sign him. Although Dwayne refused to retire from football, it was clear that his NFL career was gone before it had begun.

CHAPTER 2

INTROSPECTION MINDSET & ATTITUDE

There is so much more to Dwayne than meets the eye. We need a suitable environment to deconstruct his honesty, which contributed to his great success.

To accomplish so, we must travel back in time – approximately 25 years.

Dwayne Johnson was a professional wrestler as Rocky Maivia in 1996, before he became known as The Rock. He was a third-generation professional wrestler. Rocky Maivia was a mash-up of his father's and grandfather's ring names. He made his debut for the World Wrestling Federation (WWF), the world's largest professional wrestling organisation.

Professional wrestling is an incredible phenomenon. Professional wrestling is essentially a cross between sports entertainment and theatrical. Although the match's conclusion is predetermined, the rigorous intensity and activity in the ring are not.

Most wrestlers (and other on-stage performers) play characters, sometimes with characteristics that are diametrically opposed to their own. These characters are a gimmick designed to increase interest in a wrestler regardless of athletic skill.

Unlike in any other sport or type of entertainment, fans have the power to make or break a wrestler's career. Typically, matches feature a protagonist (historically, an audience favourite known as a babyface, or "the good guy") and an antagonist (historically, a villain with hubris, a proclivity to disobey the rules, or other unlikable characteristics known as a heel).

Rocky Maivia made his debut as "a good person," but his character was not warmly embraced by fans. On every street corner and at every venue, he was booed. During his battles, audiences were increasingly hostile to Maivia, with yells of "Die, Rocky, die" and "Rocky sucks" heard.

To be honest, the character of Rocky Maivia was created by the 'powers that be.'

In professional wrestling, the higher authorities include executive producers, corporate agents, and even the WWF's owner, the notoriously erratic Vince McMahon. They thought the best way for

Dwayne to break into the organisation was to play the third-generation superstar card. They believed that using the names of his father and grandparents would be the quickest way for the audience to accept Rocky Johnson.

Although the concept didn't sit well with Dwayne because he wanted to carve his own path, as a newcomer in the business, he opted to comply with the hire-ups' request.

He resolved to modify and remake himself after realising that things were not going well for him. Dwayne was taken off the air for the full summer of 1997 due to a knee ailment.

That summer, while healing from an injury, he dug deep within himself, reflecting and attempting to comprehend what he had done wrong and why he had been rejected. Dwayne realised that it wasn't him individually that the audience despised. They despised the idea that he wasn't himself.

"I had a realisation before returning. It wasn't so much me as a person that they (fans) disliked. It was because I wasn't being myself. I wasn't being true to myself.

Who is this guy in wrestling who smiles while getting beaten?"

Before his comeback at the end of the summer, he received a phone call from WWE owner Vince McMahon. Dwayne was given a choice by Vince. Either continue as a straight-laced nice man or become the bad guy because the audience is already booing him.

Dwayne chose to become a heel in order to give the crowd what they wanted. He asked Vince for just two minutes on live television so he could address the booing audience.

He gave the supporters precisely what they wanted when he returned.

He started referring to himself in the third person as "The Rock," and began disparaging both the audience and the other wrestlers. Rocky Maivia's character died, and from the ashes sprang a new "bad guy," who took over the wrestling world.

His new character was modelled by Muhammad Ali, with a loud and narcissistic demeanour mixed with tongue-in-cheek humour.

Within a month, The Rock had become the most popular healer. Fans flocked to the arena to boo him and watch him get thrashed. In any case, they paid for the show ticket.

To be honest, character reinvention is prevalent in the wrestling industry, but what makes The Rock unique and special?

First and foremost, this was not his first attempt at reinvention.

As described in the last chapter, Dwayne Johnson was a football player who aspired to play in the NFL before deciding to try his hand at wrestling. Throughout his college years, he was injured and underwent many surgeries. A back problem sidelined him for the entire year of his senior year.

Things were never the same after that injury.

He was undrafted by the NFL but did not give up on his ambition. Dwayne, once a highly anticipated prospect, had to realise that he isn't good enough. He moved to Canada hoping to improve his game and return to the NFL's promised land.

He trained with the Canadian Calgary Stampeders for two months before being notified that he would not be signed by the organisation.

He returned to Florida, his heart devastated and his dreams ruined. Dwayne's father brought him up from the airport because he didn't have enough money for a cab.

He was bankrupt, having only $7 in his pocket.

He went back in with his parents when he was 23 years old. History seemed to be repeating itself. Dwayne was attempting to figure out what to do next, much like he did when he was a confused and aimless teenager.

Dwayne was broke, depressed, and angry at the world as he watched his former college buddies achieve their ambitions and become millionaires.

Things became evident to Dwayne after a few months of sitting still. He was certain about the next chapter of his life. Dwayne decided to pursue a career in professional wrestling.

His father was vehemently opposed to his son entering the arduous business of professional wrestling. However, when he saw the determination in his son's eyes, he promised to train him and prepare him for the major league.

Dwayne worked hard for a few months before making his WWE debut with his newfound enthusiasm and his father, Rocky Johnson, as his trainer.

The Rock addressed the period of his life after getting cut from the Canadian Calgary Stampeders team in an Instagram post more than 20 years later.

"Playing in the NFL was the finest thing that never happened to me because it got me here.

You're going to get kicked in the shins; you're going to get the shit kicked out of you.

You have to believe that the one thing you wanted to happen is typically the best thing that didn't."

How to Reinvent Yourself

Let us first address the subject in this equation before delving deeper into the 'How-to' section. The individual.

What is your personal definition of yourself? Essentially, the entire concept of identity stems from your perception of who you are.

Finally, the concept of oneself, of who we are, is founded on the narrative that we construct based on our experiences. Our identity is formed by everything we've been through in our life, both good and bad, as well as how we interpret the world around us. An identity that embodies one's sense of self.

The trick is to not become tied to the idea of who you think you are. To put it another way, we should not become tied to the arbitrary identity we establish for ourselves.

Attachment, according to Buddhism, causes suffering.

We suffer because we are attached to things over which we have no control. Change is the only constant in Buddhism. Our youth and beauty are fleeting. People around us will die, and we will, too, when our time on Earth is up.

Accept that change is unavoidable before you begin reinventing and remaking yourself. Change is a frightening prospect for people since we are prone to maintaining equilibrium. It's human nature to desire to maintain the status quo, to retain things as they are.

Accept that the nature of all life is to evolve, and that in order to progress, you must readjust from time to time. It can be difficult to readjust when shifting from one level to the next. In reality, that readjustment and eventual identity transformation must be difficult because they can only occur when life knocks us down and we pause to evaluate it.

Otherwise, why would we feel the need to adapt and readjust if everything is fine and dandy?

The opportunity is in that readjusting.

Dwayne Johnson, for example, had to shift and abandon his identity as a professional footballer in order to become a wrestler. Similarly, he had to abandon his identity as clean-cut decent person Rocky Maivia in order to become The Rock.

Society or the environment will frequently push or impose particular roles on us. Sometimes there is a good motive behind it, like in the case of Dwayne and the Rocky Maivia figure.

It is ultimately up to us to accept or reject such roles. Create a fresh identity for yourself that commands attention. Instead of allowing others to determine your image, take control of it.

When it comes to developing an image, remember that self-talk is vital because it is self-talk that maintains the self-image. Self-talk shapes our perception of ourselves, which inevitably becomes a self-fulfilling prophecy.

When we see ourselves in a specific light, we tend to think and act in that light as well. As a result, we will obtain external validation and feedback from our surroundings and the people in them, which will strengthen our self-image.

One of life's basic realities is that whatever you portray from within, you reflect on the outside.

Now that we've discussed the significance of self-creation and identity formation, let's delve deeper into the process of doing so.

Revelation Process

Working in the personal development profession and being surrounded by some of the most brilliant minds, I have carefully observed their distinctive techniques and success patterns. Over the years, I have perfected the approach by taking the components that have worked for me and removing what didn't.

The revelation process is a series of approaches and practices that will help you acquire clarity of mind on where you need to go and who you need to become to get there.

The fact is that we live in a chaotic day and age, where we are in a constant rush to get things done. Whether it's the normal job and the responsibilities that come with it, or it's a daily to-do list, we rarely get the option of being by ourselves with ourselves and our thoughts.

If you remember the example of The Rock, when he was cut from the Canadian Calgary Stampede, he came back home to Tampa,

Florida. This was in 1995, the time where the internet and social media didn't exist.

For a few months, The Rock was left entirely alone, without the external influence and with a minimum disturbance. The only thing he could do was to sit down, contemplate and think about the next move. The same thing would happen a year later when he took time off to mend the injury, and thought of the character he wanted to develop in his WWF career.

20 years later, we live in a radically different world, where we are rarely alone and by ourselves. We are bombarded with notifications, emails, and numerous updates we need to check out. Otherwise, the planet would stop spinning.

Before you start constructing a new or improved self-image, know that the thoughts you have in your mind are not truly your thoughts. Your views are a blend of what you've heard, read online, or the influence you've been exposed by your friends, family, or your loved ones. All of those things create layer upon layer in the subconscious mind, and they regularly manifest throughout the day in the shape of our thoughts.

Before you start establishing your new self and forging your new identity, you need to situate yourself in the correct atmosphere and under the ideal circumstances to do so.

So, the first stage of getting in touch with your inner self, your genuine self, and before you start reconstructing yourself, is to clear your mind by removing the present noise.

To obtain clarity of thought, initially you need to go away from people and make sure you are by yourself. Many of us are living in major cities, and even if we wanted to, it's quite difficult to remove all the commotion and be away from people. Living in a big city has great rewards but also huge downsides. One of them is the fact that life in a huge city entails constant overpowering for all human senses. The high traffic, pollution, loud and often overpopulated neighbourhoods are playing a key part in that process of overloading senses.

Therefore, this initial step is the key one as you separate yourself from the frantic metropolis and get yourself in nature. Forrest, river, ocean, or a tiny town where natural elements are freely accessible and where you are far apart from people.

Another equally crucial stage in cleansing the mind is fasting. Specifically, technological (digital) fasting and fasting from food.

When it comes to social media, they have inevitably made our lives more connected, and there is plenty of proof of how they have improved the quality of our lives. However, there is always the opposite side of the coin.

In the last several years, we have collectively become more conscious of the negative side of social media. Movies like Social Dilemma showed the deceptive techniques of social media, where finally a person gets his/her behaviour altered and transformed.

Although I had unplugged from social media last year, and it was the best decision in my life, I am not here to preach that you should do the same. However, when you decide to go through the revelation process, you have to unplug from the matrix.

There shouldn't be any distractions, and our phone is undoubtedly the biggest one. The mind will hunt for any method to avoid performing the hard work, and getting in touch with yourself and renewing yourself is the hard work. I guarantee that the world will not end in those 48 hours (preferably 72 hours) when you are offline doing what's important for you.

Now, let's handle the food fasting issue.

Nowadays, the necessity of balanced eating is common sense. However, for many, common sense isn't common practice. Heavily processed foods are generally heavy in sugar, fat, and empty calories. Consuming lots of these foods has long been connected to an increased risk of a wide variety of health problems that might lead to heart disease or an early grave, such as obesity, high blood pressure, elevated cholesterol, cancer and depression.

Aside from the unavoidable long-term hazards of junk food and high sugar meals, the problem with this kind of diet is that it numbs and dulls the intellect, the spirit, as well as the body. Many studies have demonstrated that a junk food diet leads to anxiety, melancholy, as well as frequent mood fluctuations.

This is exactly why you need to address the diet before you go on the discovery path. This is a vital aspect of generating the correct circumstances for the revelation process. You can't reasonably construct and envisage your life trajectory if your body and mind are running on junk.

Fasting clears the mind and removes the cognitive fog.

Many different religions and spiritual philosophies promote the practice of fasting for various reasons. It's a well-known truth that many kings, emperors, and monarchs fasted before making a critical choice.

Depending on where you are at the moment before you start a full-blown 24/48 hour fast, go lightly at first. Start with intermittent fasting, when you don't eat for 16 hours, and you have a period of 8 hours where you will restore the energy by consuming good food. Proper diet means macronutrients that your body actually needs, including proteins, complex carbs, and healthy fat.

Now that you know how to clear the mind, quiet the noise, and create the correct surroundings and conditions, let's move on to other aspects of the self-creation process.

What comes next in your creative process when you've unplugged from social media and technology and given your body and mind the right fuel?

Get yourself a journal.

Journaling is one of the most talked-about and cliched personal development methods. Before you roll your eyes, understand that it's a cliche for a reason.

Keep in mind that common sense is not common practice.

Becoming a better writer allows you to become a better thinker. Arranging your thoughts on a paper in a coherent manner organises your thinking process so that you can better grasp it, which translates into more effectively communicating your ideas to yourself and others.

The major reason for writing down what's on your mind is to develop and arrange an informed, cohesive, and sophisticated collection of ideas about anything essential. In this scenario, something significant is your new life direction and identity.

Now that you understand the significance of journaling, how should you write and journal in the first place?

The beauty of journaling is that there are no hard and fast rules to adhere to. As someone who has journaled for the greater part of a decade, I can give some pointers.

Before you sit down to write and create your new identity, understand that it is a process that will demand patience. If you have never journaled before, the first thing you should do is acquire the habit of sitting down and writing down your thoughts.

When is it better to write?

Ideally, read through your notifications and to-do list for the day in the morning before opening your emails. Check in with yourself first, then with the rest of the world.

Alternatively, but equally effective, a powerful time to journal is shortly before bedtime. Rather than going for your phone and monitoring social media, use that time and energy to the discipline of journaling about your life.

How should I write?

Everything you write in your journal is exclusively for your eyes. These pages will be viewed only by you. So, when you sit down to write in your diary, the goal is to do so at the pace of thinking (or near to it). Allow your hand to wander freely, and, most essential, do not edit while writing.

What should I write?

Now that you know when and how to write, let's get to the crucial stuff:

What should you write in your journal?

Let's start there because the whole point of journaling is self-creation.

Consider your soul objectives.

Those things you've always wanted to do, attain, and experience yet have never done so for whatever reason. I'm sure you have something in mind already, but if not, allow your soul to disclose it to you.

Let me remind you that Dwayne Johnson developed The Rock by simply asking himself, "Where do I want to be in the WWF?"

A way appeared to him from there. He aspired to be a WWF champion, the company's biggest draw.

Consider and write in your journal the following questions:

1. What do I actually desire?

2. What makes me want it?

3. How will my life change once I achieve what I set out to do?

4. What would my life be like if I don't take the essential steps to achieve my goal?

5. How much am I willing to give up to acquire what I want?

Finally, consider the following:

6. Now that I've decided where I want to go, how do I get there?

7. What attitude and skill set do I need to build in order to achieve where I want to go?

Give yourself a reasonable time frame now that you have a good idea of where you want to go, how you're going to get there, and who you need to become in the process. I wish I could give you a timetable and tell you to set a goal for the next year or the next five years.

Unfortunately, it does not work that way since you are the only one who can answer the question: How long will it take me to become who I need to be in order to get where I want to go?

As a general guideline, I recommend creating a long-term plan for up to a year and setting short-term goals for the following three months. Once you've achieved your short-term objectives, sit down and review what you did, how you did it, and, if necessary, recalculate the time frame.

As a general guideline, I recommend creating a long-term plan for up to a year and setting short-term goals for the following three months. Once you've achieved your short-term objectives, sit down and review what you did, how you did it, and, if necessary, recalculate

the time frame.

CHAPTER 3

VULNERABILITY

The Rock is a massive, muscular man with a gorgeous smile and the capacity to capture people's attention in an instant. Aside from his awards and height, what distinguishes him is that he comes across as a genuinely sincere individual. Furthermore, this beast of a man has redefined masculinity, standing at 6'4 and weighing 250 pounds.

As we move away from the traditional picture of masculinity, in which a guy is expected to deal with life's difficulties by "manning up and shutting up," The Rock demonstrates that there is an alternative.

In fact, while conducting research for my book, I observed several of his interviews and discovered one consistent about him.

He is not embarrassed or afraid to discuss his failures and problems. In a few interviews, he discusses his battle with depression and how lonely he felt. As a Hollywood actor with a big audience and a platform, The Rock speaks directly to his fans about one of the most common yet least discussed mental health conditions - depression.

I was 23 years old when I was cut from the CFL (Canadian Football League) after failing to be picked by the NFL. I had to return to my parents' modest apartment in Tampa. My hopes were dashed.

You work so hard, and then someone says, "Hey, you're simply not good enough. You must return home."

You assume your life is over when you're 23. I'd gone into a profound depression, and I recall thinking at the time...I was solely interested in cleaning the walls. I took some cleanser and a rag and cleaned for days. Everything was cleaned by myself. It was the only thing I had control over.

I learnt that one of the most crucial things to understand about depression is that you are not alone. You are not the first to go through it, and you will not be the last. You frequently feel isolated and as if you are the only one.

I wish I had someone who could simply pull me aside and tell me, "Hey, it's going to be okay."

One thing to keep in mind. Maintain that essential quality of faith. Have hope. There is something wonderful on the other side of your grief.

After approximately a month and a half of living in that small flat, I received a phone call from a coach who informed me that I had been cut from the squad. He said he wants me to return and try again. I hung up the phone after telling him I'd think about it.

"You're going to do it, right?" remarked my father.

I replied, "No. I believe I'm done with that. My instincts tell me I'm done. I want to work in the wrestling industry."

"You're throwing it all away," he said. It's the worst decision you'll ever make. You are destroying your career."

"Maybe," I answered as I stared at him. Maybe I'll be no good, but I know in my heart that I have to do this. "I need you to train me or not train me."

My father rose to the situation and mentored me. It turned out to be one of the most memorable chapters of my life. Remember that there is something wonderful on the other side of the agony."

Dwayne Johnson returned to his parents' residence in Tampa, Florida, a few months before receiving that call. He couldn't afford a cab from the airport and had to contact his father to come pick him up. During the voyage, Dwayne reached into his pocket and pulled out his wallet, which he described as one of his lowest points in life.

He had a $5 bill, a $1 bill, and some change in his wallet. He rounded it up to seven dollars. A man who had recently dreamed of millions of wealth and great success, and who was so close to realising that goal, had to wake up and confront reality.

He was bankrupt and despondent.

If you told Dwayne at the time that his lowest point in life would one day serve as a springboard for his multimedia production company, he'd probably punch you across the face.

Life, on the other hand, surely writes the most compelling novels, as The Rock alluded to when he launched Seven Bucks Productions. In just a few years after its founding, the company has grown into a movie industry behemoth, producing unique content for television, film, emerging technologies, and digital networks.

Hold on to that underlying element of faith, as The Rock stated, and remember that on the other side of sorrow comes something wonderful.

Furthermore, Dwayne's '7 bucks moment' became his personal message to his admirers and followers. This inspirational story reminds us that even when life knocks us to our knees, it is not the end of the path. On the contrary, it's only the beginning, and as long as you're breathing, you have what it takes to get up and change things.

The underlying message that his supporters connect with is to be nice and caring to themselves first.

When it comes to the traditional notion of masculinity, empathy was traditionally designated for women and feminine energy. The Rock demonstrates that there is no meaningful connection when there is no empathy.

Human connection is firmly embedded in our being, our DNA. The link gives our lives meaning and purpose. We are wired to feel linked from a neurobiological standpoint.

However, you will never feel that connection until you have empathy. You can't have empathy until you're prepared to first be sympathetic to yourself. You must be vulnerable in order to be sympathetic to oneself.

Fans in the WWF, as well as the general public, are drawn to The Rock. People connect with him and his message, and they perceive him as a true, authentic human being, despite his status as one of the world's biggest movie stars.

He appears real and authentic because he has accepted vulnerability.

Contrary to common opinion, vulnerability does not imply being emotional or sobbing in public. Embracing vulnerability entails allowing yourself to open up to others and express your ambitions, thoughts, challenges, and insecurities, even if it means risking ridicule and rejection.

Being vulnerable is standing firm for what you believe in and refusing to budge, regardless of the opposing power, political repression, or worry that even your closest ones would not understand you.

What we can learn from The Rock is to convey your tale with all of your heart. Allow yourself to be who you are rather than who you believe you should be. To do so, you must embrace vulnerability completely. It's not pleasant, but it's necessary. What makes you vulnerable is also what makes you beautiful.

All of the trials and tribulations you've previously faced are what make you who you are. Your battle scars are a badge of honour for you.

Vulnerability has a negative meaning since it denotes weakness, submissiveness, and a lack of ego. Vulnerability is frequently associated with danger, jeopardy, or risk.

Being vulnerable in the face of the world, on the other hand, is not a sign of weakness. It is a superpower in comparison because being vulnerable requires guts. The courage to express your truth is what sets you free and allows you to not just grow, but also to fully experience life.

Dwayne was an angry and confused boy in 1987, long before he became known as The Rock. The main reason he was such a problematic adolescent was because of what was going on in his family at the time. The family relocated to Nashville, Tennessee, a few months after being evicted from their house in Hawaii.

''I knew my parents had problems with their marriage at that time. I'll never forget it, it was around 1 o'clock in the afternoon. We were at the restaurant and they got into it. They got into a very big fight. Not physical but just really loud arguing.

My dad had a car at the time, and they got into that car. My dad was driving and my mom was in the passenger seat. I got in the car that my mom just drove, the family car. I already had a licence at that time, at 15.

We are driving down I-65, a major interstate that runs through Tennessee. I am watching them drive in front of me, and all of a sudden their car starts swerving. I can clearly see that they are arguing.

My old man makes the hard right, he gets on the shoulder in the gravel road. My mom gets out of the car...I'll never forget it.

She has a glazed look over her eyes that I have never seen before. She walks right into the middle of I-65 and continues to walk down into the oncoming traffic.

My heart stopped.

Horns were blowing and cars were swirling out of the way. I got out of the car and I grabbed her and wrestled her over to the side of the road. I don't remember what I said to her, I remember she didn't say a thing.

At that moment, one of the greatest lessons I've ever learned was how precious life is and how in an instant it can all go away. It changed me.

The irony is…My mom has no idea that it even happened. That is the irony but also the beauty of it. She doesn't remember anything. Thank God. ''

Consider the things life has taught you the hard way.

It could be a nasty breakup, a failed business, or the death of a loved one. If you haven't already, try to see each of those experiences as a learning and transformational experience that helped shape you into the person you are today.

We frequently conceal the aspects of ourselves that are the hardest to accept, primarily because we are terrified of the change that may result from acceptance. To be vulnerable means to overcome the most formidable foe – Fear.

If you simplify the emotion and concept of fear, you will rapidly grasp the unavoidable reality about fear. Fear is nothing more than a fiction you tell yourself about something that hasn't happened yet and probably won't happen. Fear is a projected worst-case situation in the future that prevents you from doing what is best for you.

CHAPTER 4

SELF-AMUSEMENT

Pro-wrestling was at an all-time high in terms of viewership and popularity in the late 1990s. Professional wrestling, in fact, was becoming a popular cultural phenomenon. Many wrestlers have found their way to the big screen, making their mark in the Hollywood film business. As a result, formerly uninterested audiences would swarm to arenas or turn on the event and watch on television. They were captivated after that and quickly became enthusiastic admirers.

There were numerous great wrestling personas throughout the golden era, but one stood out above the others.

By the end of the twentieth century, The Rock had become the WWF's hottest product. The Rock was captivating both inside and outside the ring, far distant from the Rocky Maivia days. One of the most important components of pro wrestling is the entertainment factor, and The Rock excelled in this area. His promos were legendary, and they are still lovingly remembered and regarded as a gold standard in the wrestling profession more than 20 years later.

Throughout his wrestling career, The Rock was known for his many unique catch phrases that stayed with the crowd and pleased fans for years.

The Rock had a feud with Ken Shamrock in 1998. Ken arrived at the WWF as "The World's Most Dangerous Man," and he was a true badass in his own right.

Despite the fact that the rivalry was brief, it was remembered for the hype and what The Rock said to Shamrock. During one of their matches, The Rock stated that he would "Lay The Smackdown" on Ken. The crowd reaction was tremendous, as usual, and the slogan quickly became part of The Rock's insult repertory.

A year later, WWF will launch a new show in order to extend their market share and crush their competition. Their major competitors, WCW (World Championship Wrestling), were struggling, and in 1999, Vince McMahon decided to establish another weekly wrestling show. With their established RAW show, the WWF had a winning formula, and it was time to put an end to the television ratings war once and for all.

What is the title of the new show?

Smackdown.

The first edition of Smackdown aired on August 26, 1999. The show went on to become an instant smash and is still running today. On the 20th anniversary of the Smackdown, The Rock offered a personal tale about how he came up with the slogan on his Twitter account.

"Fun fact, I told Vince McMahon in 1998, "I'm going to use the word 'Smackdown' tonight in my promo."

What does that mean, he wondered? I stated it meant I was going to whoop some ass. He burst up laughing and exclaimed, "Say it!" The rest, as they say, is history!"

Merriam-Webster dictionary formally accepted the term "SmackDown" in 2007. To be honest, The Rock did not coin the phrase; it has long been used by newspapers and publications. However, the word was not typically employed as a compound word; instead, it was pronounced "Smack Down."

In addition to naming one of the best continuing wrestling shows, his slogan "Know your role and shut your mouth" was utilised as the title for two wrestling video games released in the early 2000s. The wrestling/gaming community regards "Know Your Role" and "Shut Your Mouth" as video game classics.

Take a look at it...

He not only made history in the ring, but he also established his legacy in world history. Video games and the WWE Smackdown show will live on long after he is gone.

The Rock made history, but he did it while having fun and embracing the self-amusement mentality. Even back then, he understood that in order to entertain and connect with an audience, he had to first have a good time.

Another fascinating story from his wrestling days is the origin of one of his hallmark movies, People's Elbow. The noise in the stands was deafening every time he did this move.

Triple H, another hugely successful wrestler, recently revealed the origins of this technique. He said that a popular technique was nothing more than The Rock's ploy to make another wrestler laugh and "break character" during a match.

The wrestler in question is the Undertaker, a legendary figure whose career spanned more than 30 years. Anyone who watched wrestling at the time, even if only rarely, will be familiar with the Undertaker character. The Rock, according to Triple H, was just having fun that evening, and while he couldn't get 'The Deadman' to break character and laugh, he hit the jackpot with the audience.

The Rock focused on his acting talents during his first term with the organisation (1996-2004), because the goal is to entertain the audience at the end of the day. As important as physicality is in the business, professional wrestling is all about people and tales delivered in the squared circle.

He honed and practised his comedic timing, which aided him later in his Hollywood career. Although he was mostly cast as an action hero over his career, The Rock would occasionally take chances with the comedy genre, resulting in mostly positive reviews and even better box office statistics.

In 2017, he appeared in three blockbuster films that grossed over $2 billion.

Baywatch was one of the films.

That picture deservedly received a special award at the Razzie Awards, which are given out yearly to the year's worst films. When The Rock found out, he taped a special greeting for his followers and critics.

"It's Oscar Sunday, and I'm super excited and proud of my friends who are nominated." I'm rooting for you guys to win the gold.

I'm also pleased because I just found out that I, too, will be taking home the gold tonight, albeit not an Oscar, but a Razzie.

But here's the cool thing: The movie was so horrible, they really had to establish a new category. I'm not kidding, that category, the new category, is 'A Movie So Rotten You Eventually Fell in Love With It.

I'm not joking.

That is, the shit sandwich you ate was so terrible that you gradually came to adore it."

Not everything in life will turn out the way you planned.

You may put in all of the effort required to create something remarkable and still have people tell you that your work is mediocre.

The Rock figured out what self-amusement is and how powerful it is. At the end of the day, you need to live life to the fullest while having fun.

The Rock's "self-amusement comes first" mentality is what makes him authentic, and more importantly, what makes him lovable and endearing. Despite the overwhelming loud criticism and hostility, he has an incredible ability to perceive the positive. He took what was valuable to him, rejected the rest, and went about his business.

His following film, Jumanji 2, was a major box office hit, grossing over 950 million dollars against a budget of roughly 150 million dollars. The true relationship between The Rock and veteran comic Kevin Hart was one of the film's highlights.

The couple had previously starred opposite one another, but this film cemented their on-screen connection as well as their off-screen friendship.

The Rock provides us a simple yet frequently overlooked life lesson. Because our time on this earth is limited, why not have fun while we're here?

How to Engage in Self-Amusement

The Rock's ability to really have fun and amuse himself is a huge part of his magnetism.

Let us now discuss self-amusement and how it relates to charm. At the end of the day, you should live life to the fullest while having fun.

Before delving further into this topic, let's first define what isn't self-amusement.

Self-amusement is not the same as self-deprecation.

Never undervalue yourself, your accomplishments, or the lessons life has taught you the hard way. Never lower your brightness to allow others to shine. Those who utilise self-deprecating humour to relieve social tension or even as an icebreaker are common.

Never lower yourself in order to lift others up.

You don't necessarily have to be funny or behave like a comedian to entertain yourself. It can take numerous forms, ranging from academic and philosophical debates to political discussions to simply being foolish.

Self-amusement is a skill, but it's also a state of mind, and our minds have no bounds. Be imaginative and imaginative. You can entertain yourself by making up strange stories and role-playing. If you find yourself at a networking event, make it your aim to meet at least ten individuals. If you have a friend with you, challenge him or her to see who can meet the most people.

When my best buddy and I need to settle a disagreement, we have a simple process.

A classic game of rock, paper, scissors.

Although our ritual dates back many years, we still play it anytime a major or minor choice must be made and we are unable to reach an agreement. A decision such as who gets the next round or who gets to use the restroom first.

The winner, most significantly, gets to "earn" his triumph and bragging rights.

It sounds foolish, and it appears to those on the outside to be just as ridiculous. Consider two mature men playing a "life and death" game of rock, paper, scissors in the midst of a pub, while everyone around us shout for their choice.

There are numerous methods to enjoy fun at any given time.

Everyone around you will sense your vibe if you are having fun and enjoying the moment. People will think you're more appealing since you make them feel wonderful.

The principle of self-amusement is both difficult and rewarding. It's difficult to begin practising, so take little steps. You don't have to start singing karaoke right away. You don't have to sing, but pick anything that interests you.

Initially, my default self-amusement principle is to observe others.

The first ten minutes of any social gathering are spent observing the atmosphere and individuals around me. I'm looking for a sense of place: the layout, the exits, the bar, intriguing individuals and their location. Who knows, maybe I'll see a familiar face among the crowd.

If I'm in a bar, I'll try to make friends with the bartender so I don't have to wait for a drink every time I need one.

In contrast, if I'm in an unknown place, such as a new pub or club, I'll spend a few minutes attempting to make friends with a bouncer or security.

Curiosity Mindset

Another technique to enjoy yourself in a social scenario is to entertain thoughts and ideas that contradict who you think you are. Simply said, the self-deprecating attitude might help you see the other side of the coin. This is especially crucial when it comes to topics on which you already have strong feelings.

Curiosity in a discourse can manifest self-amusement.

Curiosity about the other person, their point of view, and how they came to believe what they believe in can help you connect with them on a deeper level. Even if you disagree with their opinions, you can understand and appreciate the person behind those ideas and convictions.

You will occasionally come across someone who has an entirely different set of views and ideals. If religion is an important part of your life and identity, conversing with an atheist whose life is ruled by science may feel daunting and fruitless.

Politics is another contentious issue for many people. Nowadays, it's tough to have a genuine political discourse. It appears like it is only a matter of time before the discussion devolves into a furious debate.

Self-amusement keeps you from falling into the "I am Right and you are Wrong" trap, especially when it comes to sensitive matters like religion and politics.

Although there are many other topics to discuss in a discussion, why would you pass up the opportunity to learn more about the person in front of you? The benefit of having challenging but significant conversations is that you learn about yourself in relation to others.

You don't have to change who you are or even agree with them, but the want to learn and understand, paired with the ability to absorb information without passing judgement, is what allows others to open up to you and finally trust you.

There should be no bounds and restrictions when it comes to self-amusement and having fun, unless your actions are causing harm in any shape or form to anyone around you.

CHAPTER 5

CONVICTION & CHARISMA

The Rock, who was 29 at the time, decided to try his luck in Hollywood in 2001. According to his own admission, he was inquisitive and passionate about film, and when the opportunity arose, The Rock seized it.

Although he had previously appeared in cameo roles and small parts in television series and films, The Scorpion King was his first starring role. Dwayne Johnson was bitten by the acting bug and understood exactly what he wanted to do with his life.

By the end of 2001, The Rock knew he had accomplished everything he had ever desired in professional wrestling. Multiple-time champion, the biggest superstar, and possibly the most popular wrestler in wrestling history. Although he remained with the company for a few more years, making intermittent appearances, the corporation (now renamed WWE) went a different path with a much stronger emphasis on entertainment.

Dwayne was off to a new goal of conquering the movie industry, with a new era of wrestling on the horizon and fresh developing superstars.

The Rock was clear about what he wanted to accomplish in his life and profession. His objective when he moved to Hollywood in 2002 was to have a long-lasting, powerful film career. His ambition was to become a box office celebrity whose presence in the film would entice audiences to see it. His ambition was to be Hollywood's number one box office draw.

Many critics and so-called experts forecasted him a successful career in action films because he came from the world of professional wrestling. They also predicted that his career would last a few years before slipping into obscurity, as had all previous professional wrestlers.

Despite making a splashy debut in Hollywood, earning $5 million for his first major part in 2002's The Scorpion King, his path to superstardom was anything but smooth.

Once inside the Hollywood machine, he rapidly grasped the harsh reality: You must submit to current standards and accept being moulded into what Hollywood requires. Dwayne had to separate himself from professional wrestling, lose The Rock moniker, and cut back on his workouts because he was too large for the industry.

The Rock had an important meeting with his agency in 2010 to discuss the next steps and overall direction moving ahead. At the time, he believed his career was on the verge of sinking into darkness and, eventually, oblivion. However, if we look at his filmography up to that time, we can see that his films were solid action-packed and entertainment-driven pictures. The Rock, on the other hand, desired more and believed he was capable of more.

The Rock was unique back then, as he is now, and there was no roadmap for success in Hollywood for a guy who was 6 '4, 250 pounds, half black and half Samoan.

At the meeting, The Rock delivered a speech to his staff in which he attempted to emphasise the importance of potential.

"I need everybody in the room to have faith and put our best foot forward—that just because we don't see it in front of us doesn't mean it can't be done.

They looked at me like I had three heads—and I've got a big-ass head anyway, so you can only imagine"

It wasn't in a positive way, either. I felt that."

The Rock made a decision that changed the trajectory of his life and career: He fired everybody on the spot.

"I said, you're gone—thank you for your efforts, but everyone is gone, clean slate. I'm going to put people around me who are not only hungry to win and hungry to succeed, but more importantly, have the faith and understand the value in possibility."

Despite going against Hollywood's flow and perhaps jeopardising his future career, The Rock was always guided by his strong convictions. One of his core principles is to be real while appreciating your background and everything that has brought you to this point. For far too long, he felt he was attempting to fit into the pre-existing mould of the harsh film industry and the way things are in Hollywood.

The Rock has now decided to defy convention.

He returned to the squared circle in 2011 and went on to become a WWE champion for the second time. His popularity rose about this period. WWE ratings skyrocketed, and The Rock's bond with his wrestling fan base was stronger than ever.

He was the first celebrity to recognize that the tide was changing and that the power was going to social media due to the ability to communicate directly with fans. He'd go all in, and The Rock quickly became one of the world's most influential movie stars.

The Rock's ambition for his film career has always been to have longevity rather than rely solely on popularity. He believes that his success in Hollywood can be linked to his education in the industry. He did everything he could to study everything there was to know about the Hollywood business from the ground up.

He became immersed in all parts of filmmaking, including acting, directing, producing, and scriptwriting. The Rock grew increasingly involved with executive level producers, as well as the marketing and promotional components of a film. He understood that if he took the time to learn the industry from the ground up, he would be a far more valuable asset.

He acquired a new agent just a few months after firing his last one, signing with the prominent WME (William Morris Endeavor) firm.

He also collaborated with his ex-wife, Danni Garcia, who ran her own consulting firm. They founded Seven Bucks Productions to help The Rock transition from a performer to a businessman. Beginning with Baywatch in 2017, the firm went on to assist in the production of all of Dwayne's subsequent big films, including Jumanji, Rampage, Skyscraper, Hobs & Show...

Furthermore, Seven Bucks Productions is participating in a number of other planned projects, indicating that Rock's business and entrepreneurial ventures are thriving. His fan following is constantly rising, and he currently has over 217 million followers on Instagram, 15 million on Twitter, and 5.5 million on YouTube (as of 2021).

His resolve to always put the audience first is probably the most important factor for his 'explosion' on social media. The Rock discussed his film career and the inner philosophy that inspires him in an interview with Rolling Stones magazine in 2018:

"No one's going to see me play a borderline psychopath suffering from depression. I have friends I admire, Oscar winners, who approach our craft with the idea of 'Sometimes it comes out a little darker, and nobody will see it, but it's for me.' Great.

But I have other things I can do for myself. I'm gonna take care of you, the audience. You pay your hard-earned money – I don't need to bring my dark shit to you. Maybe a little – but if it's in there, we're gonna overcome it, and we're gonna overcome it together.

Going back to my wrestling days, the number-one goal in all those towns, from Paducah, Kentucky, to Bakersfield, California, was always to take care of the audience. You find that today in anything I do. Never send an audience home unhappy."

His belief in what he does and what he wants to achieve is unshakeable.

The film Rampage was planned to have a considerably harsher finish. The Rock insisted on rewriting the script, citing his personal philosophy as well as his expertise of his audience. The Rock and studio execs apparently had an emergency meeting after the situation worsened.

"I don't like a sad ending. Life brings that shit – I don't want it in my movies. When the credits roll, I want to feel great.

My problem is I have a relationship with an audience around the world.

For years I've built a trust with them that they're gonna come to my movies and feel good. So every once in a while, you have to drop this card, which is: You're gonna have to find another actor. We need to figure something out, otherwise I'm not gonna do the movie."

They eventually came to a compromise arrangement, but everyone involved acknowledges that The Rock had the right instinct and made the right decision.

Another of The Rock's convictions is to demand perfection and professionalism not only from himself but also from those around him. Multiple rumours surfaced in 2016 concerning a brawl between

The Rock and his co-star, Vin Diesel, on the set of The Fate of the Furious.

Although it was later reported that the dispute was simply verbal, it was clear that Diesel's behaviour and attitude on set was the underlying cause of The Rock's problems. The Rock even publicly chastised Vin for his lack of professionalism. Since then, the hatchets have been buried, but this incident demonstrates that The Rock is unwilling to compromise his ideals and convictions.

Charisma

The Rock's authenticity stems from the strength of his convictions. The ability to convey those beliefs is what makes him so charismatic.

There is a lot of misinformation floating around about charisma. Many people believe that charisma is a divine gift bestowed onto a person at birth. If you watch Dwayne Johnson's interview from the turn of the century, he nearly appears to be a different person than he is today. Very soft-spoken, with a serious face and scant smiling that became his signature over time. When comparing previous interviews to the most current ones, it's clear that Dwayne Johnson honed his magnetism.

But how can you become your most charismatic self if charisma is something you either have or don't have?

There is no one-size-fits-all approach to charisma. Charisma is not a one-size-fits-all quality. According to Wikipedia, charisma is defined as "compelling attractiveness or charm that can inspire devotion in others."

A charismatic individual first and foremost understands himself or herself. That is a person who employs his or her charm not just to elicit loyalty from others, but also to persuade them to take action for the greater good. That greater good can be as simple as motivating someone to make a positive change in their lives through a single conversation at the correct time and place.

Having stated that, charm results from great communication and interpersonal skills. We must agree that mastering your charisma is achievable because these talents can be learnt and improved.

All of The Rock's previously described personality traits, such as Introspection Mindset, Vulnerability, Self-Amusement, and his articulation of his Convictions, contribute to his charm.

However, there is one more aspect of communication that, when done effectively, makes all the difference.

In a previous chapter discussing vulnerability, we discussed the need for empathy. As previously stated, The Rock redefines modern masculinity since, by all accounts, he is extraordinarily compassionate towards everyone he meets. There are several personal stories from various production helpers, camera operators, and extras on set about how The Rock remembers their names and personal details.

What is the requirement for empathy? It is paying attention.

There is a widespread misperception regarding the value of listening these days. Unfortunately, many people confuse hearing what the other person says with actually listening.

Listening is more than merely hearing what the other person says and planning your next words. No, we're talking about the power of listening with purpose, with the goal of comprehending the other person.

Whether it's a friend, a family member, a coworker, an employer, a neighbour, or even a live wrestling crowd. One of the reasons The Rock was so successful in the wrestling industry was that he would pay attention to the reactions of the audience throughout his matches and promos.

I believe The Rock was born with an innate tendency for empathy. Given that he spent the majority of his formative and adolescent years with his mother, while his father was largely away attempting to find the next wrestling gig.

However, once he broke into the wrestling industry, young Dwayne received career and life-changing advice from an unlikely source. Sheik of Iron.

Iron Sheik was a world-famous wrestler and former bodyguard for Iran's Shah. He was a popular wrestler in the 1970s and 1980s, and when he spotted young Dwayne in the locker room, he took him aside and gave him guidance. The Rock is still relevant today:

"Keep your fucking mouth shut when you come in. If you're gonna be good in this business, then learn how to keep your mouth shut and your ears open, and when you get in the locker room, you just listen to everybody else."

And it was great advice. You can apply it wherever you go.

Hollywood, for instance.

How to Listen Intentionally

1. Concentrate on Learning and Understanding

The most crucial thing to have before every interaction is the proper mindset. The mindset of learning and understanding as opposed to simply responding and waiting for your chance to speak.

In most circumstances, people require good listening rather than good speech.

Keeping this in mind will assist you in steering the conversation in the appropriate direction. A path to knowing about the other person.

2. Give Your Complete Focus

Your attention is one of the most valuable gifts you can give to others, regardless of the scenario or circumstances. Whether you've just met someone or are conversing casually with a friend.

Many individuals believe that body language is an important aspect in any interaction.

One thing to remember is that the body is and always will be a servant of the mind. In other words, if your aim is to learn about others, you will use open body language and deliver the impression that you are listening to the other person.

Instead of focusing on all of the body language strategies you need to utilise and putting them in the proper order, here is something that any of us can simply attain. In a conversation, you should never do this.

When you're chatting to someone, don't use your phone.

Nothing kills a two-person relationship faster than a smartphone. The number of people that do this on a regular basis astounds me.

Taking out your phone sends a strong message that something other than the current engagement is more essential. Please excuse yourself if there is an emergency. Otherwise, Instagram alerts will continue to appear after 10 minutes.

As a general rule, if you want to be intriguing, you must first be interested. Aside from being a gift to others, your undivided attention in the conversation is one of the best investments you can make in yourself.

Remember, the more you pay attention, the more information you will receive.

3. Demonstrate That You Are Paying Attention

When it comes to human contact, one of the most crucial skills to cultivate is active listening. Engaging in a discussion and asking questions is the quickest approach to demonstrate that you are listening.

There are no correct or incorrect answers. Only individuals who work or do not work are considered.

The best questions are those that demonstrate your eagerness to learn more about the subject at hand.

There are other strategies available, but "Linking" is one of the most effective.

It all comes down to repeating or rephrasing what the other person said before and connecting it with a follow-up question or statement that verifies and supports the linked notion.

Doing so in the middle of a conversation conveys a message to the other person that you are paying attention and care. Unfortunately, not many people have such an effect.

Even while asking questions is the quickest method to learn, a discussion should not be mistaken for an interview.

So don't make it a succession of "yes or no" questions for the sake of asking them. Feel free to share your thoughts and opinions in order to make the debate as lively as possible.

4. Hear the Meaning (rather than the Words)

If you pay attention during a discussion, you will notice that different topics elicit different emotions from the person you are conversing with. Hear the meaning behind the words. Once you've done that, stick with it. Find out what's causing that feeling if at all feasible. Knowing what excites someone and why is useful knowledge for making social bonds.

Remember the subjects that elicited a favourable emotional response from the other person.

You only need to recall the highlights of the conversation, not the complete chat. Those highlights are the topics that elicited the feeling.

Make a mental note of it because you'll need it for the following and last step.

5. Follow through and follow up (Connection Bridge Principle)

The final and most often overlooked step. Also, the most important, especially if you know you'll encounter that individual again and that the last chat wasn't the last one.

This is one of The Rock's strengths (he supposedly knows the crew's names, respects everyone as an equal, and remembers to inquire how their children are doing months later).

Let's be honest.

A follow-up is required regardless of how well we left an impact or how much someone liked us.

People have a tendency to forget. People are less likely to recall how much you cared and how good you made them feel as time passes between conversations.

A connection bridge principle bridges the gap between the last time we spoke with someone and the present moment. Pick up where you left off with the highlight from the last interaction. Use the highlight of the talk as a conversation starter if it was about fitness. Bringing up the preceding highlight will usually elicit the same joyful response from the other individual.

It's also a wonderful opener, so you don't have to rely on old-fashioned small talk.

The contents of this book may not be copied, reproduced or transmitted without the express written permission of the author or publisher. Under no circumstances will the publisher or author be responsible or liable for any damages, compensation or monetary loss arising from the information contained in this book, whether directly or indirectly. .

Disclaimer Notice:

Although the author and publisher have made every effort to ensure the accuracy and completeness of the content, they do not, however, make any representations or warranties as to the accuracy, completeness, or reliability of the content. , suitability or availability of the information, products, services or related graphics contained in the book for any purpose. Readers are solely responsible for their use of the information contained in this book

Every effort has been made to make this book possible. If any omission or error has occurred unintentionally, the author and publisher will be happy to acknowledge it in upcoming versions.

Made in United States
North Haven, CT
31 October 2024

59707369R00046